A souvenir guide

Cheddar Gorge
Somerset

Nick Hanks

🍂 **National Trust**

A Wonder of Nature

Cheddar Gorge is the most dramatic feature of the Mendip Hills. Tropical seas and ice ages, flowing waters and clashing continents all worked over millions of years to create it.

The gorge has been an attraction for hundreds of thousands of years. Rightly it has been judged to qualify as part of the Mendip Hills Area of Outstanding Natural Beauty and also a Site of Special Scientific Interest.

The varied cracks and folds of the gorge are home to a vast diversity of wildlife. Half the British species of bats and butterflies live here. Numerous plants that are scarce or rare elsewhere thrive here. This landscape enabled the survival of ancient woodland from 8,000 years ago, and grassland plants from before that. There are species that grow here and nowhere else, such as the Cheddar pink and the Cheddar whitebeam (see pages 24–25).

It is also home to two culinary firsts: Cheddar is the birthplace of that world-famous cheese; and here was found the only evidence of prehistoric cannibalism in Britain. The earliest complete human skeleton in the country, Cheddar Man, was found in Gough's Cave (see pages 8–9), as was some extremely rare Ice Age art.

An unusual landscape

Cheddar Gorge is the most studied 'karst' landscape in Britain. The term comes from the German version of the local word *kras* for the landscape of the Škocjan Caves Regional Park in Slovenia.

Karst landscapes are shaped on the surface and below by water dissolving the bedrock, usually limestone, dolomite, or gypsum. Only about a tenth of the world's land is built of these alkali, dissolvable rocks, with their different soils and thus distinctive plants. These landscapes vary across the globe, from the conical hills of the Guangxi Province of China to the razor-sharp Pinnacles of Borneo, to the clints (blocks) and grykes (cracks) of Yorkshire. Here at Cheddar are some of the highest inland cliffs in the country, soaring straight up above the visitor to 137 metres, with spectacular caves beneath.

Opposite Britain's deepest gorge has created unique conditions for wildlife

How the gorge was formed

The rock that forms the Mendip Hills is mostly carboniferous limestone, which is primarily composed of the skeletal fragments of marine organisms. This was laid down at the bottom of a shallow tropical sea that covered most of Britain 360–320 million years ago.

At the end of the Carboniferous and beginning of the Permian geological period (250 million years ago), the continent of North America collided with Europe. The limestone was pushed up forming hills twice their current height. They stood in a desert and slowly eroded down to about their present shape during the Permian and Triassic periods (260–210 million years ago). The valleys of the Mendips would have been

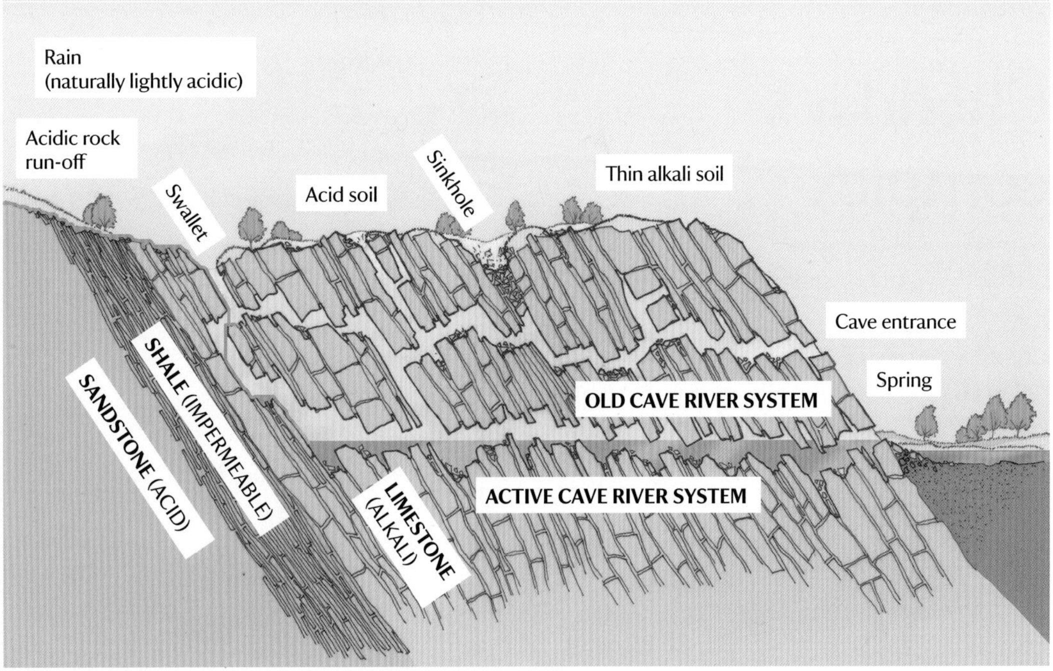
Rain
(naturally lightly acidic)
Acidic rock run-off
Swallet
Acid soil
Sinkhole
Thin alkali soil
Cave entrance
Spring
OLD CAVE RIVER SYSTEM
ACTIVE CAVE RIVER SYSTEM
SHALE (IMPERMEABLE)
SANDSTONE (ACID)
LIMESTONE (ALKALI)

Above The rock of the gorge was formed millions of years ago below a sea that once covered the area

Right Diagram showing how acidic rainwater worked its way into the dissolvable limestone over millennia to form Cheddar's caves

baking in the desert sun with small dinosaurs skittering about after prey. What rain that fell would have drained away through the naturally permeable limestone.

The Mendips were then 'fossilised' as they were buried beneath the sea. This Jurassic sea formed more limestone to completely cover the hills. Some of this covering still survives on the east end of the Mendips, and some fossils of corals and shells can be seen in the rocks of the gorge.

Eroded by ice

After further millions of years the ancient hills of the Mendips were exposed once more. Then two or three million years ago, ice began to work on shaping the hills and creating the gorge. The ice and permafrost filled the joints of the limestone making it unusually impermeable to water. So the water from the periodic melting of the ice or snow upon the hills would have run across the surface forming the 'dry' valleys and flowing through the gorge. The gorge deepened as conditions warmed. The water worked its way into the rock, forming river caves. Over time the water worked its way further underground, forming new layers of caves below until they reached the level they are at today. It was once thought the gorge was made from an enormous cave that collapsed, however the shape of the gorge is typical of river valleys.

Dissolved by acid

The limestone of Cheddar Gorge is extremely hard but easily dissolved. Rainwater is naturally slightly acidic. Water flowing off the exposed acidic Devonian sandstone at the core of the hills is made even more acidic. The water dissolves the limestone as it works its way through cracks in the rock and opens them up. At the larger openings, called 'swallets', whole streams disappear below the surface. Caves eventually form and some of the dissolved rock gets redeposited, creating the famous cave formations of Cheddar (see page 8).

The water also interacted with the Devonian sandstone and formed deposits of lead, mixed with silver, arsenic, zinc and iron ores, which were first mined here by the Romans.

Cheddar's complex

Cheddar Gorge is part of an interconnected network of valleys and cliffs, typical of a karst landscape. Formed from the dissolution of soluble rocks, it's characterised by barren, rocky ground, caves, sinkholes, underground rivers, and the absence of surface streams and lakes.

The gorge is connected at Black Rock to three dry valleys. Long Wood and Velvet Bottom are both accessible via footpaths. The longest valley has Cliff Road running through it. The surface streams disappear down holes, or swallets, before they can reach the valleys, hence they are dry. However, Cheddar's valley network drains most of the plateau and when the rain is heavy the ancient river returns to the gorge. A notable flood on 10 July 1968 saw a torrent of muddy water sweeping down the gorge, flooding shops and homes.

Where water once ran

The road through the gorge follows the path of the former river that shaped it. Though here the typical 'S' meander of a river has been rendered far more dramatic by the interconnecting vertical spurs of hard rock. From within, the gorge feels impressively tight and narrow, but from the cliff-top walk it is the width of the gorge that impresses. From above it can be seen that the cliffs to the south are vertical, rough and mostly 100 metres or more high. By contrast, the cliffs to the north are smoother and have a gentler angle reflecting the natural layers in the limestone.

What lies beneath

There are two types of cave in the gorge formed between 1.2 million and 350,000 years ago. Most are small caves amongst the cliff walls of the gorge. These were parts of extensive cave systems that have been lost as the gorge was cut more deeply. Below the gorge is a series of cave systems one above the other. Gough's Cave is the most impressive and important. It consists of three levels of caves formed by the underground river that now rushes through the lowest level under the show caves. Each cave level corresponds to a radical change in climate.

Man-made marks

Not all of the cliffs in the gorge are natural; some
are the result of quarrying mostly in the late 19th
century. Quarrying ended dramatically in 1906
when it caused a major rock fall that blocked
the gorge. This was not the first time this had
happened, but it led to a call for the cliffs to be
taken into public ownership. These stone scars
have now been weathered, blending in with the
natural cliffs.

Apart from building, one of the principal uses of
limestone has been for making lime. This was
done by heating limestone in kilns. It was a smelly
and smoky process. The limekilns are mostly
19th-century but a well-preserved example from
the 1930s can be found at Black Rock Quarry.
Lime was used in many products including
mortar for building, disinfectant, water
purification and paper-making. One of lime's
principal uses was for improving acidic soils for
agriculture. Before lime production there had
been few farms on the top of the Mendips.

Left The limestone cliffs
known as the Pinnacles

Above Black Rock

Cave dwellers

People have been drawn to caves for all sorts of reasons: ritual, adventure, secrecy, temporary shelter or a permanent home. At Cheddar the caves have a surprisingly long and full history.

The earliest evidence of people here is the simple mammoth carving in the wall of Gough's Cave dated to 14,000 years ago. The caves preserve the remains of other animals from this time: the bones of woolly rhino, hyena, lemming, brown bear, wolf, horse, red deer, reindeer and saiga antelope.

By 12,000 years ago people were living in Gough's Cave. In the climate of this icy time a cave was markedly warmer than outside. During excavation, human remains were found amongst the animal bones. Close examination of the bones revealed cut marks on the skulls and that the long bones had been deliberately smashed. They looked as if they had been treated in the same way as the surrounding animal bones. This is the first authenticated discovery of cannibalism in Britain. The defleshing of the bones may have been done out of a wish to ease the passing of the person's spirit in to the next world. They may have eaten some of the flesh to take on some of the qualities of the deceased, or merely as a source of nutrition from the extracted bone marrow. This was not the result

Above Formations in Gough's Cave

Right A skull with face bones removed to create a cup

Cheddar Man lives!
In 1997 DNA was extracted from the teeth of Cheddar Man. DNA from mouth swabs was also taken from staff and pupils of Kings of Wessex School in Cheddar. The results revealed the remarkable fact that Adrian Targett, a history teacher, shared the same mitochondrial DNA; Cheddar Man had a relative still in the area over 400 generations later!

of desperation brought on by hunger, as there were plenty of deer bones amongst the remains.

During the warmer climate after the ice melted, around 9,000 years ago, a man was buried in Gough's Cave. This hunter-gatherer was discovered in 1903 and called 'Cheddar Man'. He had taken a blow to the forehead, which did not kill him directly, but led to an abscess that might have been the cause of his death. He was in his early 20s. He had amber beads with him, including one that may have come from the Baltic.

Always returning

The caves continued to be used on occasion for centuries after. Early farmers in the Neolithic period, which in Britain was around 4000–2500 BC, made offerings in some caves but were too afraid to go very deep. Some Iron Age (800 BC–AD 100) people also lived in the caves; at Read's Cavern they were entombed in a rock fall. Even in the Roman era (43–410 AD) the caves were visited; in one cave on the Mendips, there was a coin counterfeiters' den. One of the last people to live in a cave in Cheddar was Welshman Pride Evans and his family in the early 1800s. He was the keeper of the Cheddar Pound, where stray animals were kept until their owners paid a small fine. The cave still bears his name.

Early tourists

The gorge was an ancient route up onto the hills, but it only attracted visitors in its own right from the 18th century. The visitor experience was similar to that of today: admiring the soaring cliffs, enjoying subterranean thrills in the caves, then browsing gift shops and sampling some of the local produce.

The Romantic period that began in the 18th century drew intellectuals into nature, where they would celebrate beauty and its effect on the mind, body and soul. The gorge inspired some to speculate on how it had formed: a catastrophic earthquake or perhaps the collapse of a vast cavern. One visitor was Reverend Richard Werner, a friend of the Romantic poets William Wordsworth and Samuel Taylor Coleridge, who described the scene as follows: 'The vast abruption yawns from the summit down to the roots of the mountain, laying open to the sun a sublime and tremendous scene – precipices, rocks, and caverns, of terrifying descent, fantastic forms, and gloomy vacuity.'

Enterprising locals

Visitors' musings were often interrupted by the villagers of Cheddar trying to sell them rock formations, crystals, or the seeds of the Cheddar pink. Others would eagerly recommend a tour of their particular cave, causing arguments with those extolling the virtues of other caves. These caves were often their homes too. They were not the 'show caves' we see today, but were small with few surviving rock formations and reached

Cheddar. The Pinnacles. Sept 26. 1905. from Ma

by a scramble up the side of the gorge. Below them the river was dammed to power numerous mills. Hanging over the scene was noxious smoke from the limekiln below Lion Rock (now a coffee shop) and rock dust from quarrying.

Tourism takes off

Things started to change in 1839. In that year the first show cave was opened. It was discovered by local mill owner George Cox during road widening two years previously. Shortly after he opened a tea garden and then a hotel. The arrival of the GWR railway line in 1869 prompted further developments, including exploration of another cave in 1877 by Richard Cox Gough that eventually revealed far grander chambers.

The Cox family were not the only entrepreneurs. Roland Pavey, another local miller, created Pavey's Hill Pleasure Ground, or 'Joyland'. It consisted of his own cave enhanced with rock formations from elsewhere, tea-room and shooting gallery. To ascend the side of the gorge he built the 274 steps of Jacob's Ladder and for comfort added a dumb-waiter to bring hot meals up to the top. The finishing touch was the lookout tower built in 1908, which was replaced by the current tower in 1929.

Cheddar's architectural showpiece

As the leases on various properties came to an end the existing landowner, the Marquis of Bath, took over the attractions with a new company, Cheddar Gorge and Caves, to run them. There was a period of investment in facilities. Most significantly, there was the Caveman Restaurant at the entrance to Gough's Cave built for £20,000 and opened in 1934 by pioneering architect Sir Geoffrey Jellicoe. It was in the latest 'modern' style, featuring a light horizontal design to contrast with the dark vertical rock face, and a pool full of fish for a roof. The roof unfortunately leaked and was later replaced with one of solid construction.

The Kings of Cheddar
From Saxon times to the reign of King John there were royal visitors to a palace at Cheddar. In 941 AD King Edmund was out hunting after having had a row with St Dunstan. The king chased a stag towards the cliffs. It plunged over the edge, followed by his pack of hounds. Edmund, seeing his end rushing towards him, repented of his treatment of Dunstan, whereupon the horse stopped right on the edge.

Left The Pinnacles on a postcard dated 1905

Right The Caveman Restaurant designed by Sir Geoffrey Jellicoe

Guardians of
the gorge

This landscape seems timeless and unchanging. However, people, plants, animals and weather all have their effect. The landscape is living, growing and moving, even the rocks. These shifting and sometimes conflicting forces need careful management by the National Trust, the Somerset Wildlife Trust and the Longleat Estate of the Marquis of Bath.

There is mature woodland, scrub, grassland and all the stages between. If left unmanaged, all would be covered by dense woodland of the same species. Even within the woodland, management differs: some requires traditional coppicing; some requires grazing; while other areas must have animals kept out. There is also the need to maintain a mix of ages and species within a particular type of woodland. Some areas require the gradual removal of non-native trees such as conifers and Turkey oak, and invasive species such as cotoneaster need to be kept in check for the benefit of both the woodland and grassland.

Cutting the grass

Grass is kept short by the resident flocks of sheep and herds of goats. Ponies and cattle graze the dry valley grassland away from the cliffs. Around the grassland the scrub is kept back by cutting by hand. This is done unevenly to create bays and diverse microclimates for insects and butterflies. Route ways are also created to allow the grazing animals to move between areas to spread their effectiveness.

The work is all done by hand as this is no place for machinery. The heavy weight would cause damage to anthills on the level ground, and equipment would topple over on the extreme gradients. The slopes are such that sometimes workers need to be roped for safety, while other areas are inaccessible to all but climbers.

Tending the rock

Even the rock needs careful attention. Regular inspection of the stability of the rock face requires planning, so that it does not occur when birds are nesting. At times the road is closed to allow safety works on the rock face. The rock becomes loose either through the effects of rainwater freezing in joints in the rock, or through plant roots forcing their way in. Any loose rock has to be brought down and vegetation removed. Banks around the roadside help to prevent smaller stones rolling onto the roads or parked cars. The natural rubble scree slopes are an important natural habitat, so are left in place, but they do grow over in time. Then the caves themselves require protection for their resident bats alongside maintenance of facilities for the safety of visitors.

The south side of the gorge, and the adjacent farmland, have been part of Longleat Estate since it was acquired by Sir John Thynne in 1558. It is now managed by the estate's Cheddar Gorge and Caves. The National Trust acquired the north side of the gorge in sections starting in 1910. The upper part of the Cheddar complex is covered by three nature reserves – Long Wood, Velvet Bottom and Black Rock – managed by the Somerset Wildlife Trust with Black Rock owned by the National Trust.

Left The view of the north side of the gorge managed by the National Trust

The Many Faces of the Gorge

Cheddar Gorge is an extremely rare mosaic of diverse habitats, making it a haven for wildlife. So much finds a home here that is threatened elsewhere.

Below The gorge's varied terrain includes woodland, ravines and grassland; even the dry-stone walls support a host of invertebrate life

Below right Cheddar pinks clustered on a rocky outcrop

The diversity at the gorge is made possible by the varied topography: vertical cliffs, gentle slopes, and plateaus; surfaces smooth and craggy; boulders and scree; soils deep and shallow, alkali, neutral and acid.

Each of these is further modified by different aspects: from basking in the dryness of full sun to sheltering in the moist deep shade and the permanent darkness of caves. Amongst all of these ecological niches live numerous species of plant and animal.

Ravines and cliffs

Among the craggy cliffs is habitat rare across Europe called 'ravine woodland'. The most inaccessible pockets have never been touched, and so they represent tiny fragments of the vast ancient forest that covered Britain about 8,000 years ago. Its isolation has led to the existence of three unique species of tree (see page 25).

Birds such as peregrine falcons and rooks roost on the rocks. In precarious places the Cheddar pink hangs on. Even the tumble of boulders and scree have been colonised by some particularly determined and specialist plants.

Grassland and plateau

Away from the edges you will find grassland, heath, scrub and woodland. This patchwork of vegetation supports a diversity of invertebrates. The grassland in particular has many unusual species, their survival partly due to the more windswept grassland having been kept free of trees since the end of the last Ice Age.

Dry valleys and gardens

At either end of the gorge the habitat is different again. In the upper dry valleys you'll find more grassland with orchids, and woodland of diverse sorts. Along with the usual ash, yew, oak, hawthorn, blackthorn and buckthorn, there are non-native sycamore and Turkey oak. Other areas are hazel coppice, home to the illusive dormouse. To add to the mix there are some old plantations of Scots pine and larch. The larch is the only common conifer in Britain to shed its needles.

At the lower end of the gorge are the old Strawberry Fields below Lion Rock. Local invertebrates thrive in this mix of open scrub and grass. Once this area was intensely cultivated, and it is still home to a few garden escapees such as cotoneaster and wallflowers.

Blooms

Abundant plants proclaim the biodiversity of this landscape in myriad colours, shapes and sizes. Scarce, rare and very rare plants mingle together in diverse communities with more common species.

Cheddar is renowned for its plant diversity. It sits at the northern limit of many species from the south and the southern limit for many from the north. There are four species listed as threatened, 17 scarce and 15 rare species.

Rock and scree

A few plants thrive in these seemingly barren places. You will see Welsh poppy, little robin geranium, wall rue and mountain everlasting. There are ferns: hart's tongue, bladder and limestone. There are also many mosses and lichens on the rocks themselves

In the artificial scree of dry-stone walls grow maidenhair spleenwort and wall pepper. (Wall pepper has the delightful common name of 'welcome-home-husband-though-never-so-drunk'.)

Top left Maidenhair spleenwort

Top right Wall pepper

Right Green-winged orchid

Limestone grassland and heath

These two habitats intermix and include a great diversity of plants such as quaking grass, rock rose, lesser meadow rue, adder's tongue, mossy saxifrage, rock stonecrop, wood bitter-vetch, orpine, dwarf mouse-ear, spring cinquefoil, Pyrenean scurvygrass, ling heather and gorse. You'll also find orchids, two notable examples being green-winged and autumn lady's tresses.

Acid-neutral grassland

These areas often had some agriculture in the past, which has changed the soil and thus also the plants. Here you'll find English eyebright, heath bedstraw, bird's-foot trefoil and scarce soft-leaved sedge. Betony also grows here, which was used as a dye for grey hairs in the middle ages.

Acid grassland

On these fully acid patches exists a different mix again: common bent grass, tormentil, heath bedstraw, common louse wort, slender St John's wort and pale St John's wort.

Beneath the trees

Finally, in the shade of the trees grow: angular Solomon's seal, narrow-lipped helleborine orchid and narrow-leaved bitter-cress, which is said to grow in land undisturbed by people.

Clockwise from top right
Narrow-lipped helleborine
orchid; English eyebright;
betony; pale St John's wort;
autumn lady's tresses orchid

Beasts

The diversity of plant life at Cheddar Gorge leads to invertebrate diversity, with about 29 resident species of butterflies, which is almost half those found in Britain. Large animals graze the gorge, some on impossible inclines, and mini-beasts find shelter in the rocks and the cracks of the dry-stone walls. Everywhere there is variety.

Sure-footed foragers

As you walk around the gorge you will encounter free-roaming grazers amongst the cliffs and cover. The feral goats are easy to recognise. They browse a diverse diet. In summer it is the trees and scrub they nibble on; in the winter months they move on to evergreen leaves and they will even strip the bark. Some trees need to be protected from them, but the number of goats is low and the woodland is very diverse. Despite their reputation of eating anything, they do avoid some plants.

Soay sheep come originally from a tiny island in the remote St Kilda group of islands, far to the west of Scotland. Eight of them appeared in the gorge in 1992, said to have been abandoned by a trader after the Priddy Sheep Fair. They have horns, are small, hardy and as sure-footed on the cliffs as the goats. They can be either blond-brown with a pale belly and rump, solid black or brown. They keep the grass short and the invasive scrub in check. If it weren't for the sheep, grass would out-compete the flowering plants. Their light trampling breaks up the leaf litter, and creates small patches of bare earth for seeds to germinate.

A less often seen grazer is the roe deer. This deer is much smaller than the better-known red deer. It has a reddish body and a grey face with a very short tail. It is graceful but quick, so you may not see it. However, you may hear it. The males make a low grunt or bark. The females make a high-pitched 'pheep' whine in July and August to attract the males. Most of the year they live

separately on their own territories. In the book *Bambi* the deer was a roe deer without spots, but for the film version Disney changed it to a species of deer more familiar to an American audience.

Formerly frequent flyers

Most of the resident species of butterfly have a specific diet and habitat, such as ragwort for the caterpillars of the cinnabar moth, and buckthorn for the brimstone. Elsewhere in the country modern agricultural practices have led to a loss of habitat and a massive drop in butterfly numbers. Here you can experience the diversity we have lost. In sunny, sheltered places where they like to fly look out for: small pearl-bordered fritillary, silver-washed fritillary, grizzled skipper, brown argus, dark green fritillary, dingy skipper, green hairstreak, marbled white and chalkhill blue, amongst many others.

Creepers and crawlers

Even around your feet there is great diversity in the gorge. Snails are known to be picky about their habitat; the presence of lapidary, large

chrysalis and heath snails shows that this is a good place for invertebrates. The dry-stone walls provide a home to a variety of invertebrates, including the southern bristletail, a primitive insect. Many of these invertebrates provide valuable food for the gorge's slow worms, adders and grass snakes.

The lives of different species are intertwined. There is one species of woodlouse here that specialises in living in anthills, which are well established amongst the grass. Then there is the striking-looking violet oil beetle. In just one of its many life stages the juvenile beetle climbs to the top of flowers to wait for solitary bees. There it catches a ride back to the bee's burrow and proceeds to eat the bees' eggs. When the beetle first emerges as an adult, its abdomen is small and compact but, as it gorges on lesser celandine and soft grasses, the abdomen becomes distended and can extend some way beyond the tip of their wings. They can often be found sunning themselves on paths, the iridescence of their carapace giving them a purple, blue or green sheen.

Birds

Cheddar Gorge makes an ideal place for many birds. The mixture of habitats and the open spaces of the vertical cliffs and the plateau beyond give them plenty of room to stretch their wings.

Feathered residents or guests

In the winter months many of the birds regarded as resident take shelter down on the Somerset Levels. The exposed nature of the hills means spring arrives later, so winter thrushes meet returning pied flycatchers, redstart and blackcap. The blackcap's fluting song has earned it the alternative name of the northern nightingale. Bird song is easier to catch as the shady gorge delays the dawn chorus that strikes up with the rising sun.

In summer tree pipits, whitethroat, yellow hammer and willow warbler are among the species that flock to the gorge. Above the grassland skylark and meadow pipit sing in the sun. Darting between the trees and shrubs are mixed parties of tits, finches and warblers, including the grasshopper warbler with its buzzing trill.

In the autumn passers-by include whinchat, wheatear and chiffchaff.

Hunters and scavengers

Larger birds can be seen riding the wind above the cliffs. The most familiar is the ubiquitous buzzard often seen circling on thermals to gain height. These birds have a surprisingly plaintive call, like the mewing of a cat.

Much smaller and noted for its great ability to hover is the kestrel, its wings quivering while its head remains perfectly still, intent on its prey below. The larger and more powerful peregrine falcon, by contrast, hunts on the wing, chasing its prey at up to 155 mph, making it the world's fastest animal. Kestrels and peregrine falcons have declined greatly since the 1970s due to changes in farming practices.

A darker silhouette you may see against the sky with a diamond-shaped tail or perched on the rocks is the raven. The gorge is ideal for them. They are long-lived birds, typically living up to 10–15 years, although one at the Tower of London lived to 44. It is the largest of the crow family, and has a much wider range of calls. They are wily and mischievous birds, and so unsurprisingly they have entered into many stories and tales. Smaller and more numerous, jackdaws have a grey-silvery sheen to the back of their heads, and are often seen in flocks.

Opposite Pied flycatcher

Far left Blackcap

Centre left Grasshopper warbler

Centre right Buzzard

Far right Meadow pipit

Special species

As we've seen, wildlife abounds in the gorge, but there are some residents that are harder to spot. You may not catch sight of any of these but, believe us, they're here, and if you look closely enough you'll see the clues they leave behind.

Dormouse
Immortalised by Lewis Carroll in *Alice's Adventures in Wonderland,* the dormouse really does have a capacity to hibernate for very long periods. In fact, the name is derived from the French word *dormir,* meaning 'to sleep'.

Sometimes it sleeps for more than six months of the year if the weather isn't warm enough. They prepare themselves for their long winter sleep by feasting on insects, berries, buds and nuts. Delightful to us, they were unfortunately considered delicious to people in times past. In Elizabethan England their fat was thought to induce sleep.

Dormice have a distinctive bright golden back and a pale cream belly. You are very unlikely to see them as they are entirely nocturnal. However you may see evidence of them. Look out for hazelnuts that have neat, smooth holes

Above It is rare to spot the nocturnal dormouse in daylight hours

Right Far commoner is the yellow-necked mouse

Above right The greater horseshoe bat gets its name for its distinctively shaped nose

which hibernates. The yellow-necked mouse is very similar to its relative the wood mouse. This nocturnal woodland mouse is an excellent climber, eats hazelnuts and acorns. The pygmy shrew (not actually a rodent) is tiny, weighing only four grams. It has one of the highest metabolic rates of any animal, and must eat nuts, seeds, worms and insects every couple of hours.

Greater horseshoe bat

The gorge is home to 12 species of bat, half the total number of British species. The following have all been recorded here: the lesser horseshoe, Daubenton's, whiskered, Natterer's, Bechstein's, common pipistrelle, soprano pipistrelle, Nathusius' pipistrelle, serotine, noctule and brown long-eared. However one of the largest, with a wingspan of 30 centimetres, and most easily distinguished species is the greater horseshoe bat.

The 'horseshoe' of their name comes from the shape of their nostrils, which act as a dish for their echo-location signals. They actually 'shout' their echo pulses through their noses, rather than through their mouths as most bats do. The gorge's diverse habitats provide plenty of insects for the bats, which they eat on the wing, crunching through hard shells with their sharp teeth. There are, of course, plenty of caves for them to roost in, including the show caves. Look out for their droppings underfoot, then look up to see if they are hanging above you. Most other bats like to crawl into crevices.

The best time to look out for them on the wing is in the early dusk of a summer's evening. They fly quite slowly with a flutter and a short glide. They are quite harmless to us; it is they that need protection. Due to a loss of roosting sites and feeding habitats, many species of bat are rare or endangered. Consequently all bats are protected by law. The gorge has three per cent of the British population of greater horseshoe bats.

nibbled in them surrounded by angled grooves. They are excellent climbers and can spend their entire lives off the ground amongst the branches. Dormice like the variety provided by traditionally managed woodland, in particular hazel coppice. They can build round nests of honeysuckle, bark and grass in hollow trees and other sheltered places. Special nest boxes have been provided as a means of monitoring the population. When you see one – sssh! Please do not disturb their rest as you pass.

More commonly sighted are the yellow-necked mouse and the pygmy shrew, neither of

Here and nowhere else

The diversity of Cheddar Gorge's flora and fauna is remarkable – and to cap it all, there are even a few exclusive species. There are three tree species uniquely found here and nowhere else, and also a pair of 'Cheddar' plants.

Three whitebeams

Despite Cheddar Gorge being so frequently visited and studied, these three unique species of whitebeam were only discovered in 2009. They were named after where they were found: the Cheddar whitebeam, the Twin Cliffs whitebeam and the Gough's Rock whitebeam. They remained undiscovered as they all grow in very inaccessible locations, and there are few actual individual trees. However, the most important reason is that it not only takes a trained eye to tell the difference between them, but these are not the only whitebeams in the gorge. There is also the English whitebeam, the round-leaved whitebeam and the rare though not endemic grey-leaved whitebeam.

Home-grown hybrids

Unlike the three Cheddar whitebeams, at first glance the rowan and the whitebeam look like very different trees, and not part of the same *Sorbus* tree family. The rowan has a multiple 'pinnate' leaf and the whitebeam a single simple leaf with a white underside. They could not look more different. However, the connection is revealed with the similar flowers and berries they share. The rowans and the whitebeams readily hybridise with each other, creating new species such as the service trees, with leaves that are half way between multiple and single leaf shapes. And then these new species can cross yet again to create even more new species. Often these rare *Sorbus* trees are self-fertilising and so genetically identical clones. And with the individuals often numbering only tens or hundreds, it makes them very vulnerable. The creation and survival of these hybrid trees are enabled by the diversity and isolation of the habitats of the gorge.

The Cheddar two

The Cheddar pink is a well-known plant. It was voted county flower of Somerset in 2002. There have been many cultivated varieties made available to gardeners since its discovery 300 years ago. In the wild, so many of its flowers and seeds were collected for sale to tourists that some guidebooks in the 19th century declared it extinct. However, it still grows near cliff edges as well as in gardens in the area. It is evergreen and flowers in late spring and early summer. (If you miss it, you can see some flowering on the back cover and on page 15.) The flowers have the scent of cloves. Like all in the *Dianthus* group, the petals are fringed as if cut by pinking shears, hence the name.

Though the Cheddar hawkweed is one of thousands of recorded species in the hawkweed group of flowers, there are only around 50 individual Cheddar hawkweed plants. However, it is not alone. It is joined by other hawkweeds: red-tinted hawkweed, chalice hawkweed and Schmidt's hawkweed. Most hawkweeds reproduce exclusively asexually by seeds that are genetically identical to the mother plant, thus making them all clones.

There was another distinct species, called the Cheddar bedstraw, however this is now widely recognised to be the slender bedstraw which, whilst very rare indeed, is not unique to the gorge. It is part of the same family of plants as the more familiar cleavers and woodruff. Many of the plants in this group are called 'bedstraws', as their dried leaves were traditionally packed in with linen and mattresses to keep them fresh. The sweet woodruff, for example, has a scent like that of vanilla or newly mown grass.

Opposite Perhaps most iconic of Cheddar Gorge's specialised flora are its whitebeams, seen bottom left

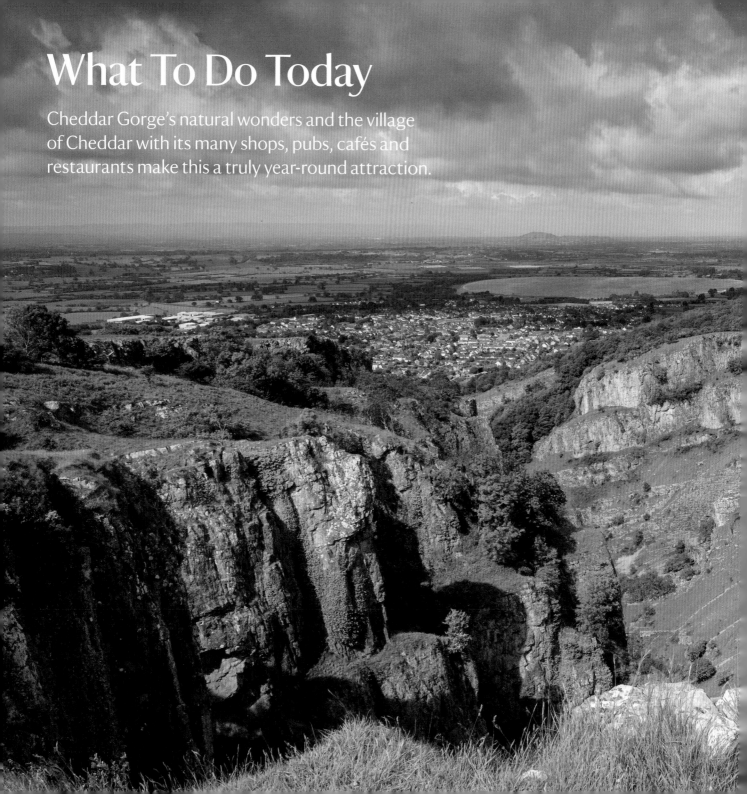

What To Do Today

Cheddar Gorge's natural wonders and the village of Cheddar with its many shops, pubs, cafés and restaurants make this a truly year-round attraction.

The soaring cliffs of the gorge are best admired from below. However, do be aware of the traffic as you gaze up at the awe-inspiring heights. The easiest way to get a higher view is to ascend the 274 steps of Jacob's Ladder, and continue on up the lookout tower. The two show caves of Gough's and Cox's provide contrasting subterranean experiences. The caves are a surprisingly warm place to explore; even in the winter they maintain a constant temperature of 11°C. Amongst the spectacular formations in Gough's Cave you will see another wonder of creation: Cheddar cheeses slowly ripening.

A taste of tradition

This world-famous cheese has been made here since the 11th century. Cheeses were usually produced *ad hoc* on the farm and hence the quality was variable. However, in Cheddar it was centralised and co-operatively organised. Thus people could specialise in making cheese, maintain the quality and develop better techniques. One of these techniques was 'Cheddaring', the practice of turning and stacking the curds until they are fully mature and have a fuller flavour. This, the only true Cheddar, is still made here today, and you can sample some on your visit.

'The best cheese that England affords, if not, that the whole world affords.'

Daniel Defoe, 1724

A glimpse into the distant past

The Museum of Prehistory has many of the important archaeological finds from the gorge, including a display on the 9,000-year-old Cheddar Man, and the skulls that may be evidence of cannibalism. Finds from the gorge are displayed, showing the development of prehistoric tools and weapons over time.

Doing Cheddar properly

The gorge has so much to offer all year round. However there will be busy periods, and be prepared for the British weather. Neither of these is anything new. In 1873 Reverend Francis Kilvert visited Cheddar. He tried to go for a meal but 'every eating-house in the village was full to overflowing'. However among his party 'a number of the foolish excursionists insisted on climbing to the top of the cliffs, got wet through and saw nothing but rain. This was what they called "doing Cheddar properly" and certainly they achieved it most completely, coming back hot, sulky, drenched with perspiration and rain, their shoes full of water, and having seen nothing but clouds, rain and mist.'

When you need it, you can escape the hustle and bustle of the shops, cafés and exhibitions by going in, under or over the gorge – climbing, caving or walking.

Opposite The beauty of the gorge feeds the soul and there's sustenance too in the village at its bottom

Above That much-loved cheese has an ages-old tradition at Cheddar

Walkers welcome

The Cheddar area offers eight walking routes, each different from the other. These were devised by Cheddar Walking, a group of local volunteers, with the support of local businesses and organisations.

Walking routes are available from the website www.cheddarwalking.org.uk or for a donation from the National Trust Information Centre near the show caves. The walks are suitable for all. There is a route around Cheddar Reservoir that is wheelchair friendly. Built in the 1930s it is an important site for thousands of migrating birds. There is another walk exploring the village of Cheddar and its long history, which could not be covered in this guidebook.

There is also the option to take a bus out to Winscombe and walk back along the route of the railway that closed in 1963. The old Strawberry Line is now a cycle and walking route all the way to Yatton mainline railway station 10 miles away. On a national scale, the Mendip Way's 50-mile route brings the gorge into the long-distance footpath network.

The path most trodden

The most popular walk is unsurprisingly the circular Gorge Walk, at 3.4 miles in length. It begins opposite the National Trust Information Centre, a little way along the track of Cufic Lane. The steep path up the hill begins from a sign on the right of the lane. The 20-minute climb through woodland and past Bake Hole Cave is stony and can be slippery when wet. In the 19th century this area was used for market gardening and growing strawberries, hence the name of the local railway line.

Once you have reached level ground you will enter a series of large areas enclosed by dry-stone walls. Don't forget to look back for some spectacular views across the Somerset Levels, towards Glastonbury Tor and the Severn Estuary. The rocky path then continues with a

There is a shorter stony ascent that weaves through the woods to take you on to the south side of the gorge. From here you have glimpses of the gorge between the trees. The path steadily increases in steepness as you descend towards Cheddar. Another fantastic viewing point emerges once you leave the trees behind, but be careful, as you will be near the edge of the highest cliffs.

When you get in sight of the lookout tower, you may either descend Jacob's Ladder or turn left and follow the unsigned path through the woods and turn right into Lynch Lane. Then turn right again down narrow Lippiatt Road. Then you will end up back on the main Cheddar road. To return to the National Trust Information Centre, turn right.

Above Cheddar Gorge offers miles of walking options all with spectacular views

Right The Gorge Walk begins with a climb and you may have to share the path with others

fence to the left and provides views of the rugged side of the gorge. This is seen at its best when side-lit by the late afternoon sun. As you reach the top of the gorge, the path goes down some steps and then enters part of the Black Rock nature reserve via a gate. This woodland path then joins a wide stony track. Turn right here towards Cliff Road. Cross this road with care.

Cavers and climbers

The rock formations of the gorge are spectacular to admire from afar. Up close, however, it is an exhilarating and challenging experience, be it hanging from the cliff face or crawling through the caverns.

Viewed from below, the soaring cliffs are both enticing and daunting in their magnificence. Those who attempt to scramble up the gorge may not get very far and can easily get into trouble. The inexperienced can dislodge rocks onto those below. A far more thrilling and safer experience can be had under expert tuition. You get to know the ropes that keep you safe, with a partner securing you using self-locking belays.

The gorge provides over 1,000 climbing routes from the easy to that typical of mountainous areas. In fact, one of the routes – the vertical 'Coronation Street' – was ascended first in 1965 by mountaineer Chris Bonnington, who went on to climb Everest four times. The rock face can be a grim place, exposed to the prevailing weather. In some conditions it is not safe for even the most experienced to climb. The climbing routes are also closed at times to protect nesting birds and to prevent loose rock being dislodged onto the busy road below. There is an access agreement between the British Mountaineering Council and the landowners to promote responsible climbing.

Opposite Cheddar Gorge has climbing routes to suit all levels of experience and daring

Above The Frozen Deep Chamber

Going underground

For the beginner Gough's Cave provides an excellent introduction to caving. Your journey into this silent domain of darkness is made easier by some permanent fixtures, but it is no less adventurous. Ladders help you down into the Boulder Chamber, and the clip-on wire is there for the traverse and crawl over the Bottomless Pit. You slide head first into the Letterbox and end up mucky but happy in the Sand Chamber. The Boulder Chamber was where David Lafferty spent 130 days in total isolation, thus breaking the world record for underground endurance in 1966.

For the more experienced caver there is the challenge of Reservoir Hole. This contains what is thought to be the largest chamber yet found on the Mendips at 30 metres high and 60 metres long. It also contains pure white pillars 5 metres tall in the Frozen Deep Chamber.

The Mendips offer many other caving opportunities. Amongst these are Rhino Rift and GB Cave, which feed water into the Cheddar cave system. Future exploration may connect these caves with those below in the gorge. The level below Gough's Cave was explored in 1985 by Richard Stevenson. Here the river that formed the chambers above now flows through 500 metres of flooded galleries.

Most of the caves in the gorge have not much to entice the caver. They are very short little passages but with intriguing names, such as Pride Evan's Attic, Bone Hole and Totty Pot. However, they are important refuges for protected species and preserve important archaeological remains. Many of the caves are gated to prevent people and animals accidently falling in. Access arrangements vary between caves, depending on the landowner and who is manages it.

Lives shaped by stone

These hills have influenced the lives of those in and around them. In return, all those lives – human, animal and plant – have shaped and continue to shape the landscape.

People have made their lives here since prehistory, dramatically changing the gorge with quarrying and by harnessing the river to power mills, or bringing about subtler changes by growing strawberries or coppicing trees.

The plateau above, once the wide-open hunting ground of kings, was enclosed and transformed into land for grazing animals. As farming practices changed, the gorge became scrubbier and more tree-covered.

Cheddar village that once welcomed Saxon royalty now receives visitors from around the world. Some have been inspired to write or make art; others explore the hills on foot, hang from the cliffs on ropes, enter the otherworld of the caves, or simply rest and take in the gorge's grandeur; some come just for the cheese. All of this has resulted in the Cheddar Gorge we know and experience today.

Not so visible is the work the local partnership does to care for it. The Longleat Estate of the Marquis of Bath, the Somerset Wildlife Trust and the National Trust are working together, steadily improving this patchwork of rare and fragile habitats to their best condition. On the one hand, they must protect the natural character of this special place from creeping urbanisation and artificial intrusions; on the other, they promote opportunities for visitors to explore and enjoy this natural wonder. Ensuring the gorge's naturalness requires a combined effort, but sharing it is everyone's reward.

Above The view at sunset over the gorge towards Cheddar Reservoir